A GUIDE TO DINOSAURS THEIR PAST AND FUTURE

By.

Rodney Cannon

While every precaution has been taken in the preparation of this book, the publisher assumes no responsibility for errors or omissions, or for damages resulting from the use of the information contained herein.

A GUIDE TO DINOSAURS THEIR PAST AND FUTURE

First edition. June 11, 2018.

Written by rodney cannon.

To my little girl Delenn, thank you for always asking questions.
I hope that you will learn that the fun is not so much in finding
the answers, but searching for them.

CHAPTER ONE FACTS ABOUT DINOSAURS

Each species is cataloged and described according to strict standards. A person who studies dinosaurs is known as a paleontologist. These scientists have found that dinosaurs likely went extinct around 65 million years ago. An asteroid collided with Earth and caused a major change in the atmosphere. That triggered a worldwide extinction phase that would change the Earth forever. That would end the Cretaceous period and give rise to new species along the way.

Pterodactyls were actually not considered to be dinosaurs themselves. They were simply flying reptiles that existed at the same time as dinosaurs. Different species of Pterodactyls emerged and would dominate the skies for millions of years. The same goes for underwater species such as plesiosaurs. Their bodies resembled dinosaurs and they would even lay eggs on the beach. But they were part of a different species altogether on the whole. Eventually, all of these reptile species would become extinct at the end of the Cretaceous period.

Herbivorous dinosaurs surprised many with their ability to thrive on the land. Brachiosaurus and Apatosaurus dominated the landscape over the years with their size. They used their long necks to reach treetops and eat leaves along the way. Their size would help them fend off predators on the land. Other herbivores like Stegosaurus would develop their own defense mechanisms against predators. They had spike tails that they could swing around at enemies. Stegosaurus likely had two brains, one in its head and another in the lower body portion. The hindbrain allowed Stegosaurus to move more adeptly on land.

The Mesozoic Era lasted from 250 million years to 65 million years ago. That is commonly referred to as the "Age of the Dinosaurs" by many paleontologists. That is because dinosaurs were the dominant species during that time frame. Famous species like the Tyrannosaurus Rex would appear during the Cretaceous era. That was a 160 million year time span that the dinosaurs dominated on Earth. That made them the preeminent species and earned them a reputation for being a dominant species overall. The dinosaurs left behind a legacy that can still be seen today. Their fossils are showcased in many museums in the world.

English paleontologist Richard Owen first coined the term 'dinosaurs' in 1842. He is credited as the first paleontologist to discuss the animals as they lived. The word is derived from a Greek term and means "terrible lizard." The term was used to describe their impressive size when first used. Little was known about dinosaurs during that time period. But all new discoveries would change the way that many perceived dinosaurs over time. Later paleontologists would describe the Triassic, Jurassic and Cretaceous time periods in full. That provided a metric to date these dinosaurs and discover more about them too.

CHAPTER TWO THE DINOSAUR'S EARTH

We do not know what the world would be like if the era of Dinosaurs still existed; would they feed on human beings or animals? Would some of them be tamed as pets as how people do today with dangerous animals such as lions and wolves and even bears?

We can only imagine what earth was like when the extinct animals existed. Dinosaurs existed millions of years ago; they are said to be fierce and vast creatures of the past. The name of the animals meant terrible lizards.

The Mesozoic era was the period when these animals were on earth; during the time to date, no human has ever seen the animals. The first evidence to prove that the animals existed were the fossils found at chalk quarry in Netherlands 1786 since then more pieces of evidence have been found in all continents, meaning that they occupied the whole earth. The era when they lived has a further division into periods and types of the enormous lizards that lived. The period includes; Triassic, Jurassic and Cretaceous. The Triassic period is 225 million years ago when all the continents of today were one landmass called Pangea. Pangea began to split into a Northern part; which is today N. America, Europe and Asia, and the Southern part which is today S. America, Africa, Antarctica, India, Australia and some parts of S. Asia. At this time the World was cold, dry. The coniferous forest grew closer to the sea level and covered the highlands. Primitive amphibians and reptiles were the animal population then, but towards the end of the period, the first dinosaur still roamed the uplands and some small mammals had appeared.

The Jurassic period was the next from Triassic; it lasted 50 million years ago. The landmass split further to form more continents both on the North and South. It is during this period that the Atlantic Ocean came into existence. The dominant land animal life was the dinosaurs. The climate was warm and humid; the mammals were evolving but were still very small.

Cretaceous period; it is the last in the era and lasted 71 million years. The continental splitting led to an age of high mountain ranges and continents took shape. Scientists have found evidence of plant life that existed such as grass, flowering plants, bees and butterflies. Towards the end of the period there were changes; increase in ocean's fish life, mammals became more significant and dominant on the land and by the end, the dinosaurs disappeared because mammals overran those that remained. Geological evidence has proved that most of the strange animals that existed during the Mesozoic era, evolved to new species or evolved to extinction.

The primary reason for the end of this time in history has been speculated upon by several geologists. One of the reasons was the fall of an asteroid; 65 million years ago. The impact of this asteroid causing a tremendous explosion. This sent billions of tons of matter into the atmosphere and left a crater over a hundred miles wide. The impact of this asteroid would have been an extinction level event for the larger of the dinosaurs. Within years it could have directly and indirectly caused the deaths of about 90% of the dinosaurs. The debris of the asteroid would have spread all over the globe and in the atmosphere, this caused severe changes to the climatic conditions of that time. It led to climate change because the debris, ash and dust covered the sky preventing sunlight rays;

thus the earth became colder. The climatic changes made some of the animal life adapt while others could not make it. The change was too sudden for many and the harsher weather proved fatal for even more. Only the extremely strong and of the proper size could exist on this new earth. It it also suggested that the asteroid would cause global firestorms. In the case of a firestorm the majority of the animals that could survive this would have been those that could have escaped to the large bodies of water. There is also a theory that the end could have been caused by massive volcanic activity. The idea of volcanoes has been the reason is a recent one. As we have recently witnessed with the volcanoes erupting in Hawaii and in Guatemala the lava is only part of the problem. The eruptions bring with them ash clouds that can suffocate any and all who come in contact with them. Then there is the sulfur that can return to earth in the form of a toxic acid rain. We are talking about a sulfuric acid rain. The levels of carbon dioxide and methane levels rise during the prolonged eruption of an average volcano. A massive eruption that could have wiped out the dinosaurs would have led to super high carbon dioxide and methane emission that in led to a massive rise in temperature.

After any of possible events competition from the remaining organisms towards the end of the Mesozoic era would have most likely been the final nail in the coffin of the dinosaur. Other animals such as mammals had multiplied by this time and now dominated the consumption of the food resources available. The scarcity of food may have led to their end.

FINAL THOUGHTS.

Break of the Pangea; at the Jurassic period, the landmass started to drift apart. Drifting of the continents naturally led to the disruption of habitat and the reproduction system. Furthermore, the land that strayed from the main continent would easily be hit by violent storms, hence eliminating some of the dinosaurs and limiting their ability to survive. A possible reason for the massive lizard extinction is self-extinction; too many of the animals evolved depleting their sources of food, most of them began to eat their eggs, most of them became sluggish and too over-sized to survive.

Through understanding the possible causes that have led to the extinction of ancient animal life, can help improve human understanding of the evolution of all animal life. What happened to the dinosaurs came without warning. Whether it came from the stars or beneath the surface of the earth it came and they did not survive it. Perhaps the greatest lesson that we can take from the fall of the dinosaurs is that we need to be prepared for all of the above.

CHAPTER THREE THE ASTEROID AND VOLCANO THEORY IN DEPTH

The fascination of every young child, dinosaurs were creatures that adapted throughout the eras, granting them millions of years free reign over the earth. This is an expansive amount of time, needless to say, much longer than humanity has ever existed or might even hope to exist. Being that this is the case, what led to the end of these awe inspiring creatures? This question has been the subject of much debate over the years, with many possible answers being proposed and rejected. Two of the most prominent theories are that of a super volcanic eruption and a cataclysmic asteroid impact. But which one seems to be the most accurate?

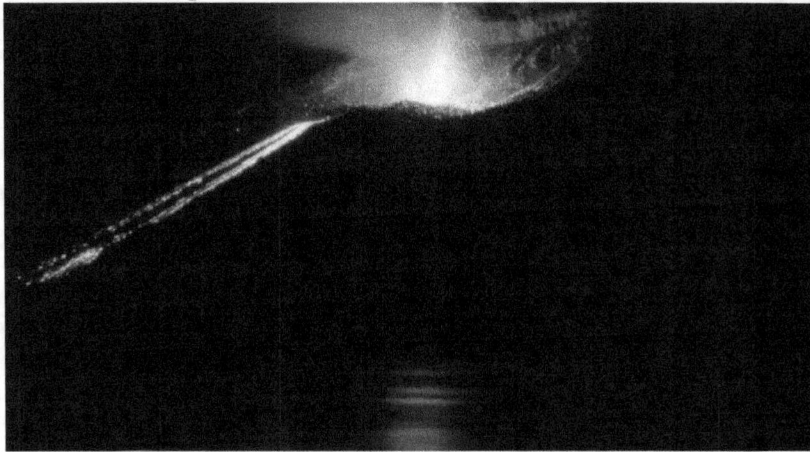

Volcanoes are potentially devastating. The lava they produce is capable of destroying towns and even completely altering the natural landscape. In addition to this, they spew ash into air that suffocates plant and animal species alike. Now imagine this destruction on a global scale, and you will understand the terrible power of a supervolcano. In the simplest terms, super volcanoes are volcanoes with the ability to produce world wide devastation. The ash clouds they create are comparable to a nuclear winter, blocking out the sun and and depriving life on the surface of sunlight. This leads to the eventual death of plant life, which in turn leads to the death of herbivores, and obviously no herbivores means no carnivores as well. This unfortunate chain of events could possibly be the cause of the mass extinction of the dinosaurs. With ecosystems completely destroyed at a very rapid pace, life would not be able to adapt quickly enough to survive the changes.

On the other hand, a cataclysmic asteroid impact with the earth also seems to be a plausible cause of the dinosaurs' extinction. Akin to a giant bomb, an extremely large meteor colliding with earth could also pose world devastating consequences. The most terrifying part is that evidence suggests this kind of world destroying impact might have already occurred. The infamous Chicxulub crater in the Gulf of Mexico suggests that it is very possible that a 110 mile wide meteor impacted into the planet tens of millions of years ago. The force created by this type of impact would be like billions of atomic bombs being dropped all at once. Obviously a devastating event of this size would produce just as devastating consequences, i.e. mass extinction.

So which one of these two events led to the eventual extinction of the dinosaurs? It probably was not either or, but rather a combination of both. Though the Chicxulub meteor was most likely responsible for initiating the end of the dinosaurs, scientists believe that massive volcanic activity that had already been happening perpetuated the inevitable end of life. The combination of these events would have so greatly changed conditions on the planet the it would have become very difficult if not impossible for the majority of life to survive.

This being said, some life did manage to live and even thrive in these treacherous conditions. Small mammals performed very well, as they didn't need as much caloric intake as the larger dinosaurs to survive. This is most likely why mammals dominate the earth today. As far as dinosaurs go, it is largely debated if any reptilian dinosaurs were able to survive mass extinction or not. However, some avian dinosaurs were able to survive, and this might be attributed to their relatively higher intelligence.

CHAPTER FOUR THE GENTLE DINOSAURS

Some of the prehistoric dinosaurs are not what you think. Scary and monstrous looking, humans can survive nearby. Not all were dinosaurs were dangerous though. In fact, there were quite a few which were believed to be the first four-legged or two-legged creatures living with humans. This dates back to more than 75 millions years ago.

These 3 harmless dinosaurs could of lived with humans millions of years ago.

Ankylosaurus

Dinosaurs such as the Ankylosaurus are hunted by dangerous dinosaurs. Plant-eaters, they were slow and bulky with their small necks and heads and less likely to attack. But, don't let their small heads fool you because of their tails are made of a hard club-like shape, it can clobber it's enemies at a good length. They can go from side to side, or from their back to front. To avoid it, these hunting dinos that want to attack must be flipped on its back and then attack the underside of this large looking beast. Most of the carnivores that were living around the Ankylosaurus did this to avoid the harmless dangerous looking dino. Many attacks are on this dinosaur. When hunted, their predators just had to flip them over to their backs and get their front side punctured. In fact, dinos such as this were plant eaters and were harmless. But because of all the plates and thorny looking body, they're known to pathologists as the "armored" dinos.

Orodromeus

These small dinosaurs were considered jumpy and active. Orodromeus means "mountain jumpers," and active. Plant eaters, they would jump from one small mountain to the next. Hence their nickname, "mountain jumping," was given to them. Co-existing with other harmless dinosaurs, and maybe humans, majority of their life was spent jumping from place to place, such as from rock to rock. They lived in North American terrain such as in Montana. They are from another relative dinosaur called the Maiasaura. Much smaller though, these "mountain jumpers" had huge thighs and small arms. Stephen Spielberg used these as the "safe dinos" in the background nearby. Their body length was about 10 feet when sprawled out. It had a toothless beak and what it did have was to crunch and grind its plants. They were light weight on average.

Parasaurolophus

One of the top harmless dinosaurs to live with humans millions of years ago is the Parasaurolophus. For those who are hunting, the Parasaurolophus may be fast but it's also one of the easiest prey to attack and kill. Taller than an Allosaurus, it can grow from 5 to 8 m tall. It's head is big and can grow as much as 1 m, plus the neck may grow as big as 2 m in height. With it being the 2nd tallest of carnivores, it even runs in water fast-like. Although, it's not dangerous at all, it's why has landed on the top harmless dinosaurs which probably lived with humans millions of years ago.

Lot of these harmless dinosaurs were plant eaters. They looked mean which was their naturally given defense against predators or hunters ready to attack these harmless creatures. Finally, with some of these 3 harmless dinosaurs whom probably co-existed with humans, they did indeed look mean looking fast and furious, but the cavemen and women who lived nearby or around their terrain like in North America, were probably more savage like.

CHAPTER FIVE THE MOST DANGEROUS DINOSAURS

For decades, people have been intrigued by dinosaurs. Also known as Dinosauria, these massive creatures roamed the planet Earth millions of years ago. The evolution of dinosaurs has been a topic which has produced in-depth research to be done by many famous scientists and archaeologists. During the days of the Triassic era, mammals were first introduced to the world and had a classification as Therapsids. Which brought about winged creatures like the pterosaurs. Then there was the Jurassic which introduced a wide variety of aquatic, marine and terrestrial life. It is also the inspiration behind the blockbuster movie "Jurassic Park".

We are going to take a look at the most dangerous dinosaurs to roam the Earth, which nobody would want to dare encounter.

1.Spinosaurus

Taking first place is the Spinosaurus, who could even defeat the notorious T-Rex. They were the largest carnivorous dinosaurs to ever walk the planet and lives over 100 million years ago. Towering at an impressive 60 ft. length, with a weight of 64,000 pounds. It's easy to see why other creatures steered clear of this monster.

2.Tyrannosaurus Rex

Next but certainly not least, is the Tyrannosaurus Rex, whose name has both Greek and Latin origins. When translated, stands for "Tyrant Lizard King", which definitely describes the T-Rex. This dinosaur lived almost seventy million years ago who reached a height of twelve feet and grew to be forty feet in length. Similar to an ostrich, the Tyrannosaurus Rex moved around through the utilization of Bipedal motion. In other words, they walked on two hind legs or limbs. However, unlike our feathered friend the ostrich, T-Rex had a bite force of 12,800 pounds. And wasn't a carnivore to be messed with.

3.Giganotosaurus

Our next contender is the Giganotosaurus, comes from the late Cretaceous period and fell under the genus of theropod. Larger than the T-Rex, Giganotosaurus had a metabolism similar to both reptiles and mammals. Chowing down on sauropods, such as Diplodocus,Brontosaurus,Apatosaurus and Brachiosaurus. All of which, were enormous in size themselves, but couldn't defend themselves against the mighty

Giganotosaurus. Reaching top speeds of up to 31 miles per hour, it over-took prey with a swiftness unlike any other dinosaur. Therefore, getting its notorious reputation for being extremely ferocious.

4. Velociraptor

Small in stature, the Velociraptor is only three feet in height. About the size of a medium bird, such as a turkey or pheasant. However, these dinosaurs were equipped with their own natural weaponry. For instance, they had large sickle shaped claws on both hind feet and a mouth full of razor sharp teeth. Perfect for tearing apart their prey and fighting off other dinosaurs seeking to make the Velociraptor its next meal.

5.Tarbosaurus

A close relative of the Tyrannosaurus Rex, Tarbosaurus lived during the Cretaceous Period and was otherwise known as the "Alarming Lizard".

Which also got around using bipedal motion like the T-Rex. They had more than sixty teeth equipped with a special locking mechanism within the lower jaws of this beast. Making it easier for them to grab prey by surprise without any chance of escaping.

6.Carnotaurus

Just as its name suggests, the Carnotaurus is a hardcore carnivore at heart. Ironically, its name stands for"Meat Eating Bull", due to the horn like bones atop of its head just above the eyes. Which scientists think were used when battling over personal territory or during mating season. Bending their heads and ramming horns with one another. The Carnotaurus are known to of fed on both large and small prey, including sauropods.

7. Stegosaurus

Over 150,000,000 years ago during the late Jurassic period, roamed the mighty Stegosaurus. Even though a herbivore, it could take down a T-Rex on with the hardened spikes and scales upon its massive back. Their main diet consisted of various vegetation, which included shrubs, bushes and trees that would grow low to the ground.

8.Acrocanthosaurus

Otherwise known as"High-Spined Lizard", the Acrocanthosaurus had a large spiny hump upon its back composed of an extra thick layer of muscle. Fossils of this dinosaur have been located throughout the United States of America, which includes Wyoming, Oklahoma, Texas and Maryland. A full-grown Acrocanthosaurus could reach a length of 38 feet and weighed a whopping 12,400 pounds, therefore making it the largest theropod of that time period. Being an apex predator who'd often prey on ankylosaurs, ornithopods, and sauropods.

9.Dilophosaurus

A unique dinosaur with unusual appearance, the Dilophosaurus is a theropod that was around during the early Jurassic time period. They had a large crest upon their skull, which went from between the nostrils of this creature all the way up to between its eyes. Just under 25 feet in length, had a slender body frame and weighed 880 pounds.

10.Ankylosaurus

The Ankylosaurus is a strange looking creature indeed, having the appearance of an armadillo combined with a Pangolin. This armored dinosaur roamed the Western region of Northern America about 68 million years ago. Generally a slow moving creature, but was quick on their feet when sensing danger. Its front jaws were constructed of a beak, with two rows of tiny razor sharp teeth in the shape of leaves. Two distinguishing features of the Ankylosaurus were a club on the tip of its tail and bone encrusted half rings upon the back of the neck.

These were merely 10 of the "Most Dangerous Dinosaurs" who've roamed the planet Earth. There were many more left un-remarked here.

Dinosaurs Which Were the Greatest Threat to Mankind

Of course, most unarmed humans wouldn't stand a chance when face to face with a dinosaur. That is, unless it was a harmless herbivore. However, the Spinosaurus, T-Rex and Giganotosaurus, posed the greatest threat due to their enormous size. Next comes the Velociraptor, Tarbosaurus and Carnotaurus, because of the swiftness and mouth full of teeth these dinosaurs were equipped with.

CHAPTER SIX DINOSAUR HUNTING

With the Jurassic Park films revitalizing dinosaurs in our modern entertainment media, a common motif is presented: how would man fare against dinosaurs? More specifically, what methods and weaponry would we implore to track and kill these great "thunderous lizards." This is a question with more than one answer. Being that dinosaurs come in many different shapes, sizes, and temperaments, there is no one universal method that would be effective in dispatching of every single variety. However, there are certain aspects of hunting that are somewhat generalizable to all creatures, be it man, beast, or even dinosaur. Firstly, it is important to study and understand your prey before the actual hunting process commences. This involves learning track patterns, feeding habits, scat identification, etc. There is no point in trying to kill any animal, especially one as vicious as a dinosaur, if you are not even capable of finding it. Secondly, you must determine what equipment is necessary for the hunt. This could entail developing calls to simulate that of a given dinosaur, or maybe even setting up bait or snare traps to control the movement of the dinosaur. In addition, you must consider what protective measures you need to take in order to save your life from potential dinosaur attacks. Most likely, a special type of body armor that is slash and stab resistant should be utilized, as to not be torn by claws or penetrated by teeth. Lastly, a hunter would be nothing without his weapon of choice. The firearm you should select is directly relative to what dinosaur you are hunting. In all cases, it needs to be of a caliber that is powerful enough to pierce the skin and destroy vital organs. With a Velociraptor, or any smaller sort of dinosaur for that matter, a 12 gauge shotgun would probably be more than enough to kill the creature. Unfortunately, dinosaurs can range from very small to very large and a 12 gauge is not going to cut it for all of them. The bigger predators, like the Tyrannosaurus Rex, would require more heavy duty firearms to kill. A well aimed .50 cal rifle would more than likely be able to rip through that thick dinosaur hide. If you want to hunt anything bigger than a T-Rex, it might be necessary to consider something along the lines of a rocket launcher, or even a tank. In conclusion, there are certain hunting methods that can be made applicable to all dinosaurs, but the tools and weaponry you use need to be more personally tailored to the specific dinosaur you are attempting to hunt.

In closing, it should clearly be understood that in an actual contest of survival between humans and dinosaurs if the humans involved are well trained and well armed then the dinosaurs would stand no chance of survival yet alone victory and this chapter did not even touch upon the use of high explosives and or air power. Mankind is the deadliest predator in the long and bloody history of planet earth because mankind is the most intelligent predator.

CHAPTER SEVEN FROM CLONING THE FAMILY PET TO SAVING THE WOOLLY MAMMOTH

Introduction Since the 1995 cloning of Dolly the Sheep, the first ever re-productive clone of a mammal, we've been curious about the potential of cloning. Does it have real-world applications? Is it safe? Is it ethical? But now that companies like ViaGen are cloning the family pet, is the cloning of humans far behind? How exactly does cloning work, and will we be cloning the dinosaurs sometime in our future?

How Does Cloning Work?

Reproductive cloning is done one of two ways. Both ways begin with a single cell from a living creature. Could be something as simple as a skin or hair cells. At the same time, an embryo, or egg, from another animal has the DNA nucleus removed. The DNA nucleus is where the blueprint for an animal's DNA is. Scientists then take the DNA nucleus of the cells from the animal you're cloning. The nucleus can be injected by a needle, or can be injected through a strong electrical current. Every single cell in our bodies is encoded with a DNA nucleus, and it provides the blueprint for everything about you. By combining an "empty" embryo with a DNA nucleus, you can clone an exact copy of the animal.

Because of the way an animals markings are partially chosen by their environment, animal clones are not always identical to the original. They also don't retain any of the memories, skills, or personality traits of the original, any more than a child and their parents might have certain personality traits. Biotech companies warn that a cloned pet isn't going to remember a previous life. It's really just a genetic blueprint that matches your pet, just like an identical twin in humans.

Animal Cloning Viable clones are very rare. Even though the technology is becoming more and more accessible, it can take hundreds of embryos before one is viable. Some of the earliest cloning techniques involve splitting rat embryos, and artificially inseminating the rat with twins. Currently, the company ViaGen will clone a favorite aging pet for a price. Cats cost $25,000 and dogs $50,000. ViaGen doesn't explain exactly what the difference in price is, but we know that some animals are more complicated to clone than others. For example, cloning primates, including humans, is much more complex. This isn't just because humans are significantly more complex than frogs, mice, or even cows and sheep. Biotech companies like ViaGen are already regularly cloning more complex animals like mice, cows, and sheep, for medical testing and even for food. In fact, the FDA has recently declared that food products created from clones is just as safe as natural animals. But there is a key difference between primates and other mammals: Unlike many other mammal types, two major proteins needed for cell division, known as spindle proteins, are located close to the chromosomes. In many other mammals, the spindle proteins are located further away, so removing the DNA nucleus to make room for a new one does less damage. In humans and other primates, however, removing the nucleus risks damaging the proteins, which means most human clone embryos could not make it far past the blastocyst stage. Even if they could, they would be at risk for deformity and health problems which would greatly decrease the human's lifespan.

However, more recently, in early 2018, twin monkeys were born in Shanghai, ten days apart. They were cloned from a cell from one monkey, and implanted in different monkeys. These are the first known primates to be successfully cloned. Of course that begs the question, "could we clone people?" The answer is, probably not. 181 embryos were implanted with the cloned cells, and of those, only 2 surrogates gave birth to live and healthy twins. In addition to that, there are serious ethical concerns to cloning humans, to the extent that even stem cell research, which doesn't involve living humans, has faced huge setbacks due to ethical concerns.

Practical Cloning - Could We Bring Back Dinosaurs?So, if human cloning is a long way off, and cloning the family pet isn't exact, what are the practical applications of cloning today? Could we bring back an extinct species? Is there a Jurassic Park in our future? Well, that's a complicated answer.

The most basic answer is no, we can't bring back living dinosaurs. Jurassic Park works with fantastical science, in which a scientist extracts the blood of a dinosaur from fossilized tree sap that has trapped a mosquito, which bit a dinosaur. This is how we get our hands on dinosaur DNA. The trouble is, it doesn't really work. Scientists have successfully extracted dinosaur DNA from tree sap before, but the resin is porous, and it's difficult to isolate the correct DNA. Even when you can, dinosaurs were much bigger than the mammals we're currently cloning. And with the passage of time, there are bound to be gaps in the sequence. ViaGen, the company that clones pets, can't clone a healthy animal 12 days past its death, due to DNA's rate of deterioration.

Because of this, in the movies, the dinosaurs DNA is supplemented with DNA from various birds and other reptiles or amphibians. While it's true that birds are the dinosaurs closest living relatives, the truth is, we know too little about a dinosaurs genetic makeup to be able to safely bridge the gaps. Even if we could, the resulting creature would still only be a hybrid, and likely bare little resemblance to a real dinosaur. Scientists are working to clone a woolly mammoth, using DNA from its closest relative, the elephant, but it has yet to be complete. If they are successful, it will be the closest we've come to bringing back the dinosaurs. It will also mark a leap forward in the cause of de-extinction. The first successful species to be cloned out of extinction so far is the Pyrenean Ibex.

Scientists are confident that the woolly mammoth can be cloned in the future. It's not exactly dinosaurs, but it's still pretty impressive! In the meantime, apart from bringing back beloved family pets, cloning offers a practical solution to medical testing and food shortages. Best of all, like all technology it's getting cheaper and more accessible all the time. It may eventually provide the answer to world hunger, and bring back species that are long gone.

CHAPTER EIGHT JURASSIC PARK THE SCIENCE THAT INSPIRED IT

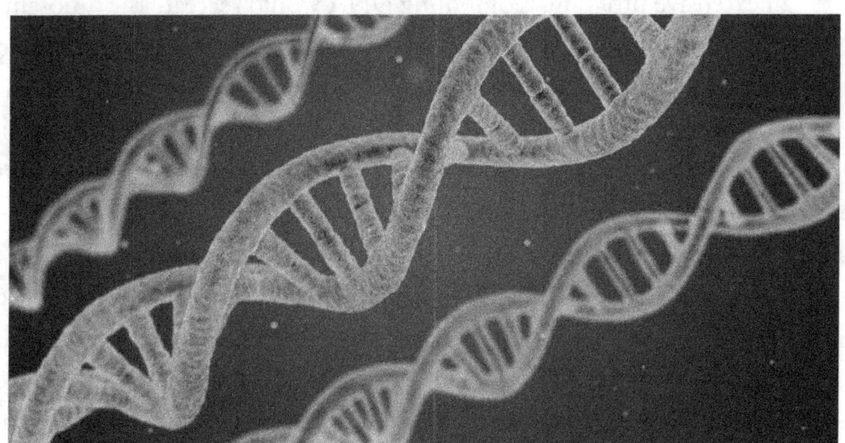

The first Jurassic Park (1993) movie thrilled audiences with large scale dinosaurs. The movie and book by Michael Crichton contained some important information to consider. The premise was that dinosaurs could be cloned using the right DNA sequence. Not too long afterwards, the first sheep would be cloned around 1999. Dolly the sheep surprised a lot of people as a cloned animal. It seemed like anything could be possible with genetic engineering now underway. Dinosaurs are ready to make a come back in a big way too. People might be curious about the concepts that are discussed in the first Jurassic Park movie.

The dinosaurs showcased were supposedly bred by harvesting DNA from amber. Mosquitoes would bite dinosaurs in an ancient era with these animals still alive. The mosquitoes consumed their blood and became trapped in amber sources as well. After millions of years, the consumed blood still contained DNA from dinosaurs. That DNA could then be extracted and used during a cloning process at the park. Eventually, dinosaurs were bred back from extinction and put on display for all to see. These dinosaurs were showcased as part of a park tour that people saw. Jurassic Park seemed like a resounding success at first.

Another idea was to include DNA from similar species in Jurassic Park. Missing DNA segments were to be replaced with strands from frog species in the area. That enabled the dinosaurs to be cloned as part of an extensive program. Combining DNA would recreate the dinosaurs in largely the same type of form. But there were some unforeseen consequences to doing that. The frogs chosen were actually hermaphroditic in the film version. That allowed the dinosaurs to start reproducing all on their own too. That kind of unforeseen consequence would be a big factor in the population of the dinosaurs.

Jurassic Park represented a big step forward for DNA science. The fictional story captivated the imaginations of millions of moviegoers that year. The book also sold well and propelled Michael Crichton to lasting fame. Follow up movies and novels proved that the formula was a definite success. People really wanted to know if DNA could be used to clone dinosaurs in real life. That has generated a lot of buzz in the media and elsewhere about the concept. It seems like genetic science is still in its infancy to today. Be prepared to follow new concepts related to DNA cloning efforts.

There are small samples of DNA from extinct species being preserved. For example, a frozen woolly mammoth has been unearthed from a tundra in Russia. That specimen is being preserved by science and reports are already coming out about it too. Some speculate whether blood and other DNA samples can be harvested from that organism. That would allow scientists to collect DNA from a species that has now gone extinct. Advanced cloning methods could prove to be useful in a number of important ways. These extinct creatures could be brought back to life using the Jurassic Park method after all.

The woolly mammoth DNA could be combined with extant species on Earth. That could include the African Elephant or the closely related Asian Elephant species. The combination of the DNA samples could allow scientists to clone a similar species of woolly mammoth. It would still retain many of its important features and will move forward with a lot of its recognized appearances. True fans of science will undoubtedly be impressed with that move. Dinosaurs may be a long way off, but other extinct species are a possibility. Try to understand DNA samples and what that means for the cloning science.

It has been over 20 years since the first Jurassic Park movie. The popularity of the series has certainly generated a lot of buzz for people out there. They are seriously discussing new aspects of the film and what that might mean. Genetic engineering has become a focal point of debate with many people. There are scientists and researchers that want to understand more about DNA in general. The movie provided an impetus to review the DNA science and what that could mean. People have taken a new look at the world of dinosaurs as it stands today.

Human cloning is another concept that is being widely discussed. That idea carries a lot of controversial topics to consider in good time as well. Dinosaurs were just the start, but cloned humans could bring in an all new debate. There are ethical questions that will need to be answered about cloning in general. People want to know where the DNA will come from for human cloning. Parents are wary and wonder whether that is the right choice to make. But the potential of human cloning has always thrilled scientists to a certain extent. They want to make the most out of an all new scientific method.

Homo sapiens are the latest in a long line of smart hominid creatures. There are extinct species of hominids that could be brought back to life as well. Neanderthals and Australopithecus are species that have captured the imagination of scientists for some time now. Neanderthals only went extinct about 30,000 years ago on planet Earth. Restoration efforts could include combinations of DNA like that used in the Jurassic Park film. That controversial idea could bring back extinct species like the Neanderthals. That will create a visualization of these Neanderthals as they once existed years ago too.

Ethical concerns will continue to be debated for human cloning. Neanderthals would make a feasible cloning subject in the future. Genetic manipulation is going to be a hot topic that many want to understand in good time. DNA is a realistic opportunity to bring back extinct species that have vanished from Earth. Some scientists would argue that the opportunity cannot be missed. But social critics might worry about the populations of animals that are created. What rights would be given to these newly created animals? Scientists would also need to care for the genetic clones. It would be hard to find the right living conditions for clones.

Don't miss out!

Click the button below and you can sign up to receive emails whenever rodney cannon publishes a new book. There's no charge and no obligation.

https://books2read.com/r/B-A-YPE-FEIT

BOOKS 2 READ

Connecting independent readers to independent writers.

Did you love *A Guide to Dinosaurs Their Past and Future*? Then you should read *On Writing A Low Budget Screenplay* by rodney cannon!

On Writing A Low Budget Screenplay will not only offer advice and rules that must be followed if you wish to craft a script that can be produced for a few thousand dollars, but how to look at your script from the view of the film maker. This book is short and to the point. It does not take more words to tell you how to write a low budget script than are actually in one.

Read more at cannondigitalfeaturefilmmaking.blogspot.com.

Also by rodney cannon

30 Days Cooking series
Cooking With Strawberries, 30 Days of Cool Recipes

BITTER WATERS SUITE
Bitter Waters Suite, Episode One
Bitter Waters Suite, Episode Two, Reasons to Believe

Blockchain Technologies
Bitcoin and Cryptocurrency

Empires Falling Short Stories
Hunting The Hand
Empires Falling, The Land of the Khan
The First Port In The Storm
Whispers From A Speaking Demon

microwave cooking

Cooking With Mic, 25 Easy Microwave Recipes and More
Desserts With Mic

PARANORMAL INVESTIGATORS
Paranormal Investigators ed And Lorraine Warren, The Enfield Polter-
geist
Paranormal Investigators 2, Amityville An Ed and Lorraine Warren File
Paranormal Investigators 3 The Exorcist, Father Gabriele Amoth
Paranormal Investigators The Collection Books 6 - 10

The serial killers
The Serial Killers, Pure Evil
The Serial Killers Collection

Standalone
On Writing A Low Budget Screenplay
Running An Online Business, Ending the Confusion
On Low Budget Film Making,Digital Film Making Interviews
Calling Vicki
The Micro Budget Film Making Collection
Cooking With Ketchup, 30 Go To Recipes
A Guide to Dinosaurs Their Past and Future

Watch for more at cannondigitalfeaturefilmmaking.blogspot.com.